Dream Weaver

Dream Weaver

A selected collection of poems

Carl D. Foggey

ISBN-13: 9780692893487
ISBN-10: 0692893482
Library of Congress Control Number: 2017911767
Carl D. Foggey, Tumwater, WA

Table of Contents

Dedication

To those that have wished to touch the stars but have lost the will to move their hands. For those who have been lost in the corridors of forever but still have the will to dream of the yesterdays that come to comfort them. For those mired in the hurt, the hate, the heartache and the habitual horror of past and present circumstances, know that there is still hope. There is a way. There is voice out in the distance that is encouraging and reassuring. Heed its message and know that you are not alone. You can still weave a dream out of the calamity and chaos. This voice is for the voiceless. This dream is for those that have lost the will and desire to do so. This Dream is weaved for you.

Hypnotized by your lines
I make love to your rhythms

Your style entices me

Your grace overwhelms me

I stand astounded
your vernacular compounded
my auditory sensory
once I played it back in my mind

My mind…
my mind still encapsulated with
your passionate prose
and your sensual stanzas I…
shutter when your words flutter
to my ear

Come here my dear
tell me again
how your verbs spin
when they twist from your tongue

I stay up late nights
immersed in your velvet verses
your satin soliloquies
do much more than please
my six senses

Your sentences
past and present tenses
played to music or a cappella
vibrates through delicate decibels

Your simplistic yet intricate sonnets
beautify ballads and serenade synonyms
I yearn to be
in-between the lines with you
poetry I think I falling in love
with you

Sincerely Yours

Sunsets

It Started With a Kiss

It started with a kiss

Sealed with a promise
of bliss that left
my tongue tied

Trying to describe
the union of
our lips

I…
drift aimlessly
trying to contain the
thoughts of what
could be if we
connected like
currents through
conduits

I…
knew it the first
time your eyes
locked paths with
mine using
nine as my compass
I devised twelve ways
to say three words
that convey
this six sense

that has me convinced
that you belong
with me

Using my third eye
to see beyond
what's before me
I explore the
curves that
hold words hostage
and watch as you
kidnap my every
quiet thought
and use my heart
for ransom

Trying to fathom
what causes me
to feel your touch
when you're not there

Gridlocked in a
blank deep stare
that I tend to
go into
when I hear you
sing your
subliminal siren song
calling me by name

at waking dawns
and midnight's eve

I weave this dream
of you and I
interlocking like
infinity signs I…
I rise at your command

Revealing the reveille
that makes time
stand still
I can feel your
skin beneath my
fingertips still
and still keep
the profile of
your smile on
the mantle of my mind
still…

I dedicate whole days
full nights
and quarters of mornings
to yearning to return
to the journey
we embarked on
the night before

Keeping score of
how many times
I can put chills
down your arms
and trace love letters
on your neck

Making more than dots
connect I...
regret spending
anything less than
a lifetime with you

Using childlike wonder
I stare at stars
hoping for dreams
to come true

Caught in the
dream catcher of night
losing sight
of dreams past

Imagining how long
will this
daydream of mine last
so all that I ask
is that I
go back to the

place where I
first experienced bliss

Mango sweet and
brown sugar covered is
the memory I go back to
when remember
how I never
felt anything
quite like this
and how it all
started with a
kiss

Forever Infinities (Next Lifetimes)

Bring to me
my days
so I can
count the hours
spent in this
love of ours
sent to me
to be
more than real

I want to feel
higher than
surreal
and appeal
to much more
than my sixth sense
I speak in present tense
because the past
is not an option

I cannot imagine
stopping any manner
of motion
that moves us
beyond this emotion
I'm hoping that
your days
remind you
of me

smiling sweetly
above thee
just to see
yours in return

I'd turn back
time
so we can meet
for the first time
again
and spend our
first kiss
in the bliss
that I pictured
back then
that is even
greater now

I vow to
dedicate my
days to come
to keeping you
from
ever leaving my memory

So vividly
I picture me
holding we
above you and I

Writing our names
in the sky
coupled with Xs and Os

Even the most high
knows our affinity
for love that he
gave me introspection
to see your divinity
as my reflection
when I pass by

The past I
see as a reminder
of what is to be
leading us to see
forever and infinity
together
taking joint steps
in this lifetime
and the next

In Dreams (with you)

In my dreams
I cling to your touch
using the night
as my covers
I slept in a bed of ecstasy
with you next to me

I dreamt that
I fell so deep
into the abyss
of your kiss
I drowned
only to have you
bring me back to life

I have visions of me
tracing your curves
and leaving my signature
on your sensuality

I have thoughts of
taking you to the edges of
time and space
without ever
leaving this room

I imagine
whispering my intentions
in your ear

just to send chills
down your spine

I want to freeze time
five minutes past midnight
so that the moonlight
highlights
your luminous skin
beneath me

I fantasize of
getting intoxicated
in your orgasms
and having hangovers
in your aftershocks
I can picture
laying you
on the tropic of cancer
as I stimulate
your prime meridian

I want to caress
your temples in the pyramids
and massage
your constellations on Saturn

We can burn incense
speaking of things
in past tense

while envisioning
things to come

I want to bathe you
in moon waves
and feed you cherries
picked from the stars

We can swim in
the waves of yesterdays
and paint silhouettes
on sunsets
sleeping softly
under moonbeams

I contemplate these things
in dreams
with you

Back In Time

Flipping through
time portals
Amazon dreams
and rainforest
mind thoughts
resurrecting love
like a refined corpse

Making love to yesterday
like it's the future
caught in a time gap
maybe my mind relapsed

I'm in your arms
stroking your first quotes
inhaling your black smoke
smiling as your
skin meets mine with ease

Smelling your hair
like an opiate cloud
back and forth
reliving tension
like it was animated suspension

I hear you laugh
"Oh God, this must be real"
orgasming my memories
clutching the sheets
like minutes refrained

One look at your eyes
and I get lost
in your lashes
just the glare of your stare
gives me back flashes

Rubbing my shoulders
thinking
"Maybe we didn't finish
the last chapter"

Look at my watch
seeing time move backwards
the sun rising at night
you turn my head to you
kissing me beautiful
I forgot why we feel apart

Lighting indigo candles
wanting to see you move
with dark back drops
my heart stops
your touching my resuscitation
not speaking a spoken word
I'm focused more
on the love we're making

I have questions
you touch my lips
with your fingertips

no need for words
the soothing sound of your bliss
filing my auditory convex

Complex
contemplating your theorems
while my soul
is multiplying in your square roots
I can't compute
this solution
this answer
not adding up

You whisper in my ear
"It's too bad you're waking up"
I reach for you
as you fade into the candlelight
I'm left with sweaty sheets
and scratches on my back
empty picture frames
and blank photo albums
decorate my room
torn love letters
and empty vodka bottles
filled with scribbled messages
saying
"Wish you were here"

Bliss of Your Lips

Bless me with your
lips but
your kiss
is far from me

Come be
as one sea
connected with
oceans of
hypnotic potions
of Love No. 3
as we flee
I fling
feathers
of forever
in the air

Queens and gods
stare
as we dare
to approach heaven
with each passionate
kiss
this passionate bliss
lists my demands
of tattooing the
sun on my hands
and Saturn
on my chest

As I sunbathe you
in each caress
and lie
engaged in
rings that propose
depth in each
breath I breathe
in the air
you leave

Coloring hearts
on my sleeve
I retrieve the
tracks your lips
left on my face
to trace how
exquisite your
kiss tastes

I stand in
the place
where you need
to be
so evenly
distributed
in my
deeply rooted
veins
that spell your
name

Speaking in
after thoughts
of passions went
and loves came
I rain forever
unto your bed sheets
and make your
legs weak

Vibrating with
the percussion
of sensual touching
lusting loving
and desiring divinity
that defines the wind
like a sweet memory

These lips that
bless me and
caress me
making my "Kind of Blue"
nights "My Favorite Things"
strumming the strings
of my soul
as your heart sings
Love: In us major

Redefining Sunsets

I dreamt
I spent nine
lifetimes with you
and through each one
each sun I saw
during my waking hour
reminded me
of you

Gaining strength from
your rays
my midnights
become days
when I'm in
your presence
your essence
illuminating every
particle

Even the very
thought of you
tears my heart in two
due east and
due west

Sunrises and sets
in my chest
where you
find rest
while within

my embrace
Can you taste
the nectar of the sun
uniting us as one?

One body…
One flesh…
During sunrises
and sets
we redefine
how love was
meant to be

Allowing you
to see how
passionately
we delve into
each other's
souls

Falling under the control
of ecstasy
while you're next to me
I see the end
of infinity
when you hold me
intimately
causing us to
glow incandescently

Fulfilling destiny
until the sun
sets on this
tapestry
that we create
tracing figure eights
on the small
of your back

I recall on thoughts that
make me envision
your silhouette
under orange sunsets
that defines a time
I'd forget
if I wasn't reminded
of your eyes when
I looked toward
summer skies
and saw you there
watching how you
compliment my sunsets

Lie To Me

Come close to my
face
and erase all notions
of doubt

Let the words
flow from your mouth
that
you need me
completely
to be the
man
that holds hands
and comforts
his lover's soul

Tell me of
dreams told
and mold me
with a silken touch
letting your fingers brush
my torso
and go
beyond my nether regions
by soothing and pleasing
what I
need not say
as we lay
chest to back

Give me that
feeling of black
magic as it
possesses
under caresses
my being
seeing what you
say
and hearing how you
play
with my desire

Igniting fires
that inspires me
to listen closely
to you tell the
ways you love me
more than days
exist in lifetimes

Tonight I'm
needing you
to speak of words
that pierces vital nerves
like
forever
infinity
together
divinity

Descend to me
with stretched wings
and hold melodic
dreams
and sing to my
ear that
you'll remain here
through blessed and
troubled times

Plant seeds in
my mind that
blossom into reality
sweet roses of
tranquility
that grace the air
so beautifully
get as close
as you're supposed
to be
and let those
sweet lips of yours
LIE TO ME

Voice of Season

Springing into dreams
where our love
seems to blossom

I often
get caught in your
April showers
and spend hours
kissing your fresh
morning dew

Lying with you
with the sun's shine
on our face
we embrace the
warmth of our
passion

Spending nights
sweating from
satisfaction
asking summer rain
to remain with us
for hours

Feeling the power
of summer solstice
the closeness we have

raises more than
my mercury .

We currently
fall into categories
of enchanted lovers
that discover
in our august events
we make love
that is heaven sent

So benevolent
that it leaves
our signatures on the
earth
conceiving a love
that gives birth
to serenity

Raising the epitome
of ecstasy
together we
freeze time for
a season

Believing that
what we posses
in winter's solstice

provides warmth
through the coldest days

The love we have
stays constant
through time spent
in seasons
of love

Visions of Dreams

I saw you
in my dreams
once again
and towards the end
I felt your kiss
on these lips
and I knew
it had to be
real

Waking up
to feel
if you were
there with me
how quickly
these dreams fade
when I enjoy
the masquerade
of intimate moments
made
in the heavens
of my mind

Slightly better
than the last time
when I
felt you so
close
maybe I'm just

obsessed with the
hope of
our lips meeting
at the 10 to 2
position
as I envision
placing my hand
on your back
ready to catch you
before you
freefall
into divinity

Beloved, you are
sending me
to places I've
never been
loving when
we're together in
my dreams

Feeling so
real it seems
I'm seeing
visions of next
days the deep
ways this feeling
penetrates my soul

I've never told
You how I
truly feel
but in my
dreams we
don't need words
so I still
speaks three words
that go unheard
but you feel them
after each deep breath
'til all we
have left is
You and I
hand in hand
Woman and Man
being as one
Again

Unbuckle

Stop…Wait
rush to the pause
that brings us closer
and even yet
still the currents
that course over
and through me
now… then
later and maybe after
I can see you
where you once were
over and underneath
my skin

I pretend that
you reside in daydreams
and days seem
so boring if I'm not
pouring every ounce
of my existence
into you...
us…

We laughed
as the storms came

We embraced as the
sun scorched our backs

We slept in interlocked arms
as the hunger
tore at our stomachs

We looked to the
Heavens as visions
of apparitions shined
smiles into our eyes
as we exchanged
baited breaths
under nights with
blackened skies
that filled my daymares

I stared into morning suns
hoping to see
a glimpse of you
there

There...
in every sun
that sets
we set our eyes upon
every sun rise and
beneath purple skies we
paint tomorrows soon come
and those that came and went
and the todays that are

forever spent
remembering the last
words I saw
and the last kiss
I heard and
the beautiful smile
I felt like
you knew what it would
mean and I struggled then
to understand now
what your touch
was trying to say

How the twirl of
your finger could cause
whirlwinds in my subconscious
The tailspin I would
dive into could
only mean two words
-Start Over-

Beginning from scratch
the feelings I'd detach
like pages of words
torn from my memory
and I tried to recite
them again but
I can't stand their sight
anymore and never will again

but I can't erase
your face that is still
stained on retinas
and my repressed memory
still holds you like
the arms of my mother
when the bad dreams
would come back again

I'm entangled in this web
of regrets and I
have yet to escape
from its grips
but it is your lips
that I still yearn
to taste again

It is the scent
of your skin
that I miss
and I wish that
the sunrise didn't
remind me of you
anymore

I wish that I
could drift into
daydreams again
without replaying the

moments we would spend
staring into eyes
wondering if you felt
as I feel and
if our eyes could
reveal what was
next to come

Take my hand and
Run...
Stop...
Wait...

Walk to the pause
that brought us closer
then and now

The still currents
are the undertow
of sorrow that courses over
and through me
now... then

Before and after
I saw you
where you once were
over and underneath
my skin
I pretend that

you still reside in
my daydreams
and days seem
so much more painful now
than what they once were
when the days were
filled with your hands
navigating fingers
over my navel
and was able to
unbuckle my dreams
with subtle gestures
and the texture of
leather and steel
would reveal
more of me

See…
Touch…
Feel
my restraint
I yearn to be
unbuckled again

Smiles in the Sky

Sweet melody
heart songs
heard in my ear
Can you tell me
which star is yours?

Sending down sweet sounds
from heaven
or so I thought it was

Being swept away
by my forget-me-nots
I tend to sway away from
your celestial windstorms

Spinning webs of
night colored colloquialisms
I am made perfect
in your sunset sonnets

Can you smile for me?
I want to see how
the stars are supposed
to shine

I want to know
how the moon is supposed
to glow

Your smile is the
precursor for
predawn days

I was told
that your tears
are moonless nights
melancholy
hidden by shrouds of clouds

Tell me how to not make you cry
I want to be enveloped
by your velvet essence
even your lunar hymns
makes me think of her

Let's go where the day
can never find us
let's spend forever nights
so I can stay in your indigo lights

I want to slumber
in your sweetness
promise me you'll
never hide again
and I promise
to always make you smile

Autumn Lady

Allowing you
to warm my cold turns
in the slow burns…
that reside
in the fire of your desire

Your love moves me
to measures
unseen
by my naked eye

Clothe me
in your kisses
undress me
in your caresses

You cause
every word
that falls from my mouth
to be poetic verses
for you

Do you
feel
when I
send shivers down your spine
just by
imagining it?

or

causing you
to moan in the dark
clutching sheets
unable to speak...
just because
I dreamed it

For me to say
I love you alone
wouldn't sound as strong
as
I'll love you forever
in time
Laying into years
your days marrying my nights
reaching heights
that would make
angels dizzy

Catch this kiss
forming on my lips
to drip onto your soul
whole
being
perfect even
with you

Promise I'll Stay

Reoccurring in my
dreams nightly

I tightly
grip unto you
pursuing you
like fleeting
memories

So vividly
I picture
us within
touch

I clutch
this dream
that I
hold dear

Wanting you
near
I fear
that after
the moonlight
my sight
loses trace
of you

So beautiful
you

make me
want to pause
the sun
leaving me
with one
delight
under midnight

I promise
that under
moonlit days
in your arms
I'll stay

Needing my dreams
to be
more than real
I feel
your fingers
trace my face
and
color love scenes
down my neck

Choosing to forget
that you
reside in my dreams
I seem to
get lost in this
beloved fantasy

Taking your hand
as we
endeavor past
love letters
and journey to
forever

Together we
manifest melodies
with the sound
of you telling me
that you'll always be
at my side

That is why
under midnight skies
I hide
to be beside
my love
that transcends days

Letting your heart
hear me when
I say that
in your arms
I'll stay

Resonations In My Mind

Causing me
to smile
in ways
that amaze
even me

Deeply
positioning myself
to be left
with options
of watching
you
parade around my mind

Oblivious to time
as long as I'm
a quarter 'til you
I'm only half past
being whole in
your grasp
for hours
on end

You send my pen
on trips
that makes my ink nauseous
no need to be cautious
throwing it to the wind

where I caught your
kiss in the first place

Remembering the last taste
of our first kiss
this passionate roulette
has missed
the point of returning
to subtle hints
catching a glimpse
of what could be

Seeing the endless possibility
of constantly
feeling your touch in my sleep
letting your fingertips seep
into my soul

Letting the overflow
of our passion
to come crashing
into our love's undertow

I need to go
where your heart
once was
so I can enjoy
your past and present
love

Taking my time to
study each and every
line of your face
and decibel
of your voice

Making my
choice words
indecisive
on whether
forever or infinity
can better
express the depth
of my devotion

I am hoping
that the sound
of my smile
resounds in your mind
as yours does in mine

Touch and Go

Touch and go
Touch and go
Touch and go to places
where there are fine lines
and familiar traces of me

Go
Go and touch
the places that I
hide so clearly
and dearly

Clutch chests like a mother's arms

Touch those intimate
and inanimate spaces
crawl through
and up over and to…

Go
Go to where shadows
hide from the dark
curl inside and died
but relied on a heart
to be touched
so touch…

Touch and go with me
and be as we

intended to be
one and become
two in search of
three ways to reach
back to nowhere
and stare at where
we first came
and explain how
we never spoke
but I still knew
your name

Go…
Go beyond the broken
bottles and hallowed morrows
that spilled sorrow
over twenty and four
gauges

Feel over me like
Braille pages
Tell of tales like
sages of how
my wrinkled lines
are ageless…
when you touch…them

Come
Come and go join me

like Tigris and Euphrates
Meet and bend
and spin days
like silk
and weave nights
like satin

Propose like
rings of Saturn
that I engage with your caress
when you touch me
I am blessed

Don't go
Don't go without
touching me first
I played every second
and rehearsed each scene
and seeing like third eye
your hand trace
my forearms
and I ...
give all
five senses
to feel warmth
since this occurred

My chest cavity
is searched for words

to explain
how I feel when
each letter of your name
falls from my lips

Touch and go
with your lips
tattooed
as a kiss
tied around my
fourth finger
so I won't forget
what made your
memory linger
in places
where I remember
names more than
faces

Let us
write love poems
in the sand
so the tide
can erase us
and make us
more than a feeling

Touch
and show more
than we're revealing

Go

Come go with me
and touch hands
like we once were
and where forgotten
dreams cannot blur
the memory
of you gently
touching my
subconscious
and caressing me
subliminally

Literally scribing
our names
on each chapter
going to where
your touch can capture
more than my attention

Please mention
our names
when you speak
to angels
tell them how
we made hour
hands move slow
and tell them how
our flesh would feel

every moment we
touch and go
touch and go
touch and go there...

Sleepwalk Talk

Slow walk dreams
portray these scenes
that often times
feel so sensual
to feel
and touch
this much
that they cause
cold blood
to rush
through my soul

This image to hold
you
is true too,
correct?

I'd expect you
to be here
slightly near me
to hear me breathe
softly in your ear
my words often
muted yet
my expression undisputed
ly
clear
ly
tell the tale

I've been chasing
in circles

See, it's hurtful
not to
alert you of
the impeding love
on the horizon
blessed by the stars
of Orion
am I
solely dedicated
to walking in step
with you
making our motions
perpetual

Dancing clockwise
and eyes gaze
at our graceful display
amazes
the absent in attendance
seeing the minutes
stand still for 60 seconds
at a time

What's the matter?
Never mind the sun's shine
this moment was made for

me and you
What do you mean
it's not true?
Do you not feel me
gently gliding against you?

"I'll miss you"
is not the expected answer
my graceful dancer
fades as the indigo
goes away
into the moonset
my slow steps
lead me out of
this scene of dreams
that remains unseen
until the dawn
of my next slumber

Respiratory Stimulation

Breathing you in
feeling you
permeate my skin
and penetrate my darkness

Occupying compartments
of my whole being
I'm whole even though
part of you
has left me
exhaling collectively
blowing stars
into midnights

The highlight of my
days is
remembering the sounds
of you breathing
gently in my ear
leaving
me with smiles
that are painted on
for eternities

I want you to
turn to me
breathing in sync
as we yearn to be

in this moment
of time
until time elapses
and collapses around us

Just listening to the
sound of
inspiration
as the expiration
of days ceased
and cause my
diaphragm to release
songs in the key of you
searching for your
seventh octave
as I stop to
smell the scent
of your embrace
inviting my face
to meet halfway
with yours

Penning the chorus
to this opus
with my focus
on filling my
lung capacity
with rhapsodies

sung in falsetto harmonies
loving how
you respond to me
inhaling serenity
exhaling tranquility

Lose Touch

Touch me in ways
that makes me remember
how the sun sets in your eyes
and when suns rise
I can find traces of you
underlining each ray
that highlights my skin

Let your fingerprint
go within to the depths
of my spirit and
finger paint
"I Love You's" all over
my soul

Sign love letters
written with the tips
of your fingers
and let each word linger
from your lips
and drip into
loosely held grips that
ever so gently
touch me
so that when
your hand embraces mine
I will forever have a time
when time ceased to matter
and the thought of having
your laughter fill the air

I breathe caused me
to smile

Touch my lips
with a kiss
that lifts my daydreams
into night scenes
of our skin tones blending
into one another
and discover hues
so beautiful that
the nightscape of blissful nights
becomes the canvas
for our passionate brush stokes

Let your hands become
as words spoke
loud enough to become
whispers
gently touching me
ever so slightly
but strong enough
for me to hear you

Let my lips
form the shape
of a heart
as I blow halos
of *"I Love You's"*
for you to put

your third finger through
and engage the thoughts
of *Here Afters*
with proposals spoken under
dreams as wedding chapels
and marry our intimacy
with eternity

Let us be
as the wind
moving with wings
of Heaven
as we touch Eden
leaving the remembrance
of forever evenings
in the breaths
of words kept
in promises heard
and embraces felt
within our touch

Keep my touch
next to your heart
and find me there
always feeling where
you need me the most
circling close
to where my head
once laid

and where hymns
for her are played
Composed of notes
we wrote under the stars
touch my hand
like this love of ours
will slip from
my grip
and please
don't let go

Floetics

Animated Suspension

Caught on the tail end of
somewhere and in between
I come to grips with
attainable dreams
that cascade over
stained glass

Moments pass as
eternities
knowing that we
mortals cast off time
like shadows
round 'bout midnight

Moonlit days compliment my
vast arrays of
incandescent luminescent
omnipresent anonymity

This melancholy soliloquy
vividly underscoring
malevolent tranquility

Freeze frame shots
of blood tinged eyes
transmit the surreal demise
of (hu)man

Held with torn and tattered
minute hands
hour glass sands
flow ever so
slightly

Tightly coming to grips with
yesterday's future intentions of
liberating arrested development
and coloring animated suspension

Dream Weaver

I can weave
you a dream
if you
just ask

Trying not
to pass
the past
I move
forward
by looking
toward my
memories

Vividly picturing
me as
He in the
3rd person
that I met
once or twice

Heeding the advice
of next life
times
sometimes I'm
constantly looking
forward to dreams
that I weave
so serene

that it seems
my subconscious
watches as I
sleep

Getting REM cycle
deep
leaving life cycles
incomplete
when I speak
in broken tongue

Leaving midnights undone
by breathing life
into the sun
spirit moving as
one

Being
second to none
third eye seeing
words sung
over drums
that comes from
the depths
of heartbeats
as hearts speak
in staccato rhythms
that resonates deep
to the soul
of me

Multiplying truth
by infinity
'til my words
equal eternity
I turn to see
the sun
call me by
first name
as I remain
in tune
with the moon
and conversing
in verses
with stars

Manifesting a mirage
that makes me
motionless
Inhaling sunsets
in my chest
and express
with each breath
that I've fallen
for you
weaving in and out
of dreams
that yearn
to come true

Conversations With Me

As I and
younger me
sat quietly
pondering why we
live in the
subconscious
and before I
could utter
a response his
head turned to me
and said
if you could
tell me anything
what would it be?

So I thought
for a moment
as he
looked on patiently
"Truth"
I said to me
and then I began
to put it clearly
to see if he
fully grasped
what I was saying

It's so amazing
how a dream
of words
coupled with
thoughts deferred
could deter
the urge
to purge my soul
if my dreams
were heard
aloud

Even now
I whisper
promises drowned
in silence
and use fingertips
to paint gifts
that a
blind third eye
can't see

Can't see why
I chose truth
over lies
as I realize that
I needed proof
to coincide my
words to you

me
'cause it's true
see
'cause I can't lie
to we

In this
circle of trust
we need honesty
to modestly walk
among the thorns
and move on
even after we
get tired

See, it's hard wired
in us to breathe
so exhale life
when you inhale truth
and tell the difference
in each sentence
you speak
because when
the truth goes within
it goes deep
so I go within
my arm's reach
and squeeze
to show me

that I believe
that what I was saying
was truth

Breathe

I live in the skin
of drums
that beat
conundrums
and cause conniptions

Where I'm from
I run to
the happiness of warm guns
and hollow my point
of view
at point blank
stare at the air
of mystique
of blood and concrete
where dandelions
grow under the feet
of the dispossessed
that catch no rest
in the nets made
for dreams
I weave to perceive
my leave of absent
mindedness is no less
than my presence
in past tense

I pass dense clouds
of hocus pocus

and fabricate my prognosis
that the dopest hypnosis
bring my daydreams
into focus I lack
attention span
deficient of
malcontent hands
I promised since
I breathed life
after birth
and left death
with second breath
taken and
forsaken so I cried out
outcries about
missing warmth
and vocal vibrations
and other gifts taken
after gestation

Homosapienated
habitually stated
words of love
consecrated
never left abated
we breathe
with baited breath
waited on He
that would return

I burn tree of life
limbs that remind
me of Him
so I hum
and beat drums
like I know
that He'll come
when I find
the right rhythm from
the depths of me
I close eyes to see
He standing there
and prepared to
inhale we
Breathe

Samo Thoughts

I create masterpieces
using pieces
of the master

I capture
the rapture
in chapters
of Psalms
manifesting Songs
in the Key
of Life
times of
written life
lines
that rhyme
in synchronized minds
provoking thought
that talk
to spirits in the wind

Passing then
becoming now
in the present
I present words
spent on
love and revolutions
of syllables
that riddle through
literal phrases

over lined
pages that
raises ink
over the surface
defeating the purpose
of penetrating the fortress

Penning up
pentameters
setting parameters
I parasail through
up and over to
askew a view
of a jaded few
in a shade of blue
that fits my mood
in indigo

Alluding to illusions
giving transfusions
of ink
proving that
"Plush safe He think"
as thoughts sink
dreams arise
to fruition

Missing the
intension we
bitching they don't
listen
as we whisper
aloud
getting lost in a
crowd of
I, me and my
vision of the third eye

See the centrifugal
spiritual slap box
with my paradox:ical
physical communication
taking ticking time
looking...waiting... I'm
using what I'm losing

Find
truth beneath
the broken lines
I unearth rebirths
of reverberations
taking hits off
constellations
sitting in deep concentration
spitting celestial hymns
while splitting Him

into Hi I'm
lost and refined I'm
lost with time I'm
lost between rhymes
I'm....
((((({{wind}}))))

Braille Teeth

Speak to me
with truth
that seeks
to be
hidden in
the forbidden
prose of words
told

Hold me like
promises kept
looking before I
step in the name
of loves
that remind me of
days when
the words I say
play back
like auto repeat

Going as deep
as forgotten memories
I vividly
picture the
touch that
I couldn't see
could it be
that I possibly
needed your hands

to tell me
all that I
needed to know?

Speak to me
slow as I
let every letter
sink in
and I pretend to
see you
through rose colored
glasses

Asking if
the past
has past us
running back
to catch the
last laugh
of us
and never let go

Let the wind
blow *forevers*
into my
never will agains
and let tomorrow
spin until then
drips into now

leaving me
wondering how
eternities slip
through lips

I forgot
that I caught
them with
a kiss
blowing it
from the tips
of my fingers
as it lingers
through the
air like
forgotten cares
as I stare
into infinities

Picturing the
end of the
regrets that I
once kept
under low breath
speaking words that
crept into
my dreams

I put familiar things
aside
and embrace the
unknown
piercing deep
like the speech
from Braille teeth
I feel what
you are saying
touching every
meaning and
conveying words
to my spirit

I hear it
when you whisper
echoes
and don't let go
when you
grab onto each one
but keep some
for safe keeping

Reaching for tomorrow
like it's right
across from you
and let these
words go right
through to

where I left
and let the
depth of
each breath
breathe and leave
signatures
on what I
perceive to be
your soul

Let me hold
or better yet
touch your
mouth to
feel what you
are saying
reading your
fine lines
and define
the truth
you're conveying

Spilled Ink On The Page

As the ink
spills onto
the page
my pen
blazes trails
seen under black light
illuminating
the tight grip
each script holds
on my soul

Searching for control
of compositions written
in fourth person
traversing on
three verses
seeing print versus
cursive

Writing her gift
onto curses
spoke into names
that burst into
flames when
I write on the
lanes these words
travel on
on notepads I babble on

in Babylon
and sing songs in the
key of Zion
as I ride upon
this train of thought

Getting off at
every stop
cause I prematurely
come to conclusions
that this pen
that I'm using
is transfusing my
soul onto pages
that raises my
A Positive
into *A Typical*
composites of
mental calligraphy
that vividly
depict monoliths
in the forms
of hieroglyphs
and lift the
spirits of dead souls
that choose writing
as their mode
of transportation

Elevating lines
above loose leaf
getting lost in speech
that navigates
through deep
vibrations
penning ruminations
that runs sentences
into images of
word on collisions
written on poetic
tapestry that happily
use words of flattery
to tragically
detach the scratch
from paper

Saving my nows
for later
I cross nouns
into faders
at 33 and one third
of verbs
that backspin
on the tip
of ink pens
that spill blood
on blank pages
leaking as I'm seeking
to find words
to save us

Traversing Time

I thought that time
had fell on
the lines of
my rhymes
and distorted
the sorted order
of syllables
that riddle through
visceral portals
of my lips

Catching the
drips of my
subconscious
onto sheets
on sale for 1 cent
per thought
after it's caught

Shaken and flipped
love sought
and bought in
nickel bags
I find my
name in tags
sprayed on decayed
facades I
poke and prod
until they crumble
like walls in Jericho

Playing in ultrasonic
stereo are
the phonics
of sonnets
spoken onto
tympanic membranes
that refrains
from keepin' it real
and peel like oranges
to reveal
the fruit
of these lips

Speaking in hieroglyphs
I lift ink
from sheets
and place them
in the heavens
so verses rain
every seventh hour
so that these
words of ours
can shower us
three times a day

The words I say
in torrential downpours
of metaphors
that manifest

into metaphysical
transitional verbs
of traditional words
that speaks in
a language
that will not languish
into the abyss
of existence
ever since
bones were
housed in flesh
I have left
the song of
my breath
into the depths
of my being

Cursing my
third eye for seeing
and my sixth sense
for feeling
the impact of the
collapse of time
onto my rhymes
as I try and find
the rhythm
between heartbeats
and break beats
as I escape

onto every
line my
mind gives birth to

Going through
raising pains
I say the name
of poetry
and she turns to me
waiting to be fed
the formula of
words said
laying her to bed
in the cradle of existence
I see her dreams
in the distance
of time
being unable
to define
what reason
my rhyme has
producing lines that's
traversing yesterdays
leaving a million ways
to come to you
once

Listening to the Wind

Spinning wind
through thin
veils to
set sail
across ecstasies

Hoping to be
one with the sun
calling me son
I become undone
under drums
that beat
the history
of my spirit's
mystery

Mystically transforming
transcripts falling
from my lips
that drip into
undotted 3rd I's

Heard cries
blend into
the 3rd verse
of my laughter
that came after
the 3rd bridge
where I hid truth

underneath
the bass line

Using the wind to
keep time
listening to
breezes construct
rhymes
that reminds me
that my muse moves
me

Deeply
digging
the roots
of my devotion
moving in motions
that twists leaves
and leaves dust in the air

As beat percuss
words
that covers mouths
watching backspins
on 12 inches of earth
crossfading birth
into life
scratching over death
playing it twice

in case you missed it
the 1st time

Witnessing the resurrection
of rhymes
words rolling back
stones
using trees as
microphones
hearing the wind
freestyle poems
that makes blades
of grass snap fingers
and rivers say
"Yo, that's deep!"

Listening to the
spirit of wind speak
I feel complete
with you and I versing
in the 3rd person

Author of Blank Pages

Rhythmically I'm supposed
to represent

A descent
that is born of the sun
speaking with native tongue
I hung verbs and similes
like strange fruit soliloquies
so vividly

I timidly approached
the throne of
grace and faced
the disgrace that still
leaves this sour taste
testing
quiet still waters
that bore boisterous
sons and daughters
that till minds unchartered

Planting in barren soil
my high blood pressure boils
at the thought of
how low our words
have sunk

Maybe still half drunk
on liquid scriptures

that seems to paint
baroque pictures
that sheds shattered glass
lacerating my feet
as I try to pass
the road of
enlightenment and perdition

I cannot forget to mention
the tension that keeps me
hyper after hours
making mortal men cower
under the pressure
not caused by trans fats
See the fact be
we commit intentional
rhymes with no fear
of the time
spent penned up
between lines
with bars bold or fine
this is the mind
of the author of
blank pages
the writer
for the unadventageous

Dominatrix

Do you see
how you entice me?

Making me lose
sleepless hours
by whispering to
me and
gently tickling my ear

I hear your sweet
voice beckoning me to
give you the attention
you crave

You've made me
your slave
I'm chained
to your demands

Keeping me in the palms
of your hands
you insure
your needs are met
your haunting words
I can't forget how
you surround me
like silhouettes

You make sure
that I can't leave
the way you satisfy
my needs
you keep me bound
by your passion

I'm lasting as long
as I can before crashing
I hear you laughing
~ *I knew you'd come back* ~
despite the self-control I lack

I relapse into your arms
once again
it started first with being
friends
and before I could begin
to notice trends
my mind started to spin
increasing with vertigo

I heard it so
clearly still
I asked you to repeat
nearly knocking me
off my feet

as my legs got weak
finding it hard to speak
you spoke

- I'm going to take hold
of your mind
and turn your thoughts to
rhyme
your emotions will only
be devotions towards me
rhythmically professing
your love
placing nothing else above
me -

And then all I could see
was me writing line after line
uncontrollably
solely penning verses
and this curse is
made worse when it hurts
to know I can never
be free
from the chains and
the pain
known as poetry

Heart Song

Speaking with breath
from the universe
I seek deep
in a verse
to find the
fine lines that
rhyme in rhythm
with my memory

I vividly picture
with closed lids
words hid
in the fibers
of my iris
seeking Isis

I write 'cause
her love song
speaks to me
beyond the
blank page
and the lyrics fade
into jade and indigo

Beats harmonizing so
sweet
penetrating so deep
I feel her vibrations
in my feet

tingling my soles
you dive into
the soul
as I let myself go

The wind sends
wax cuts and blends
that tends to
break the beat
of my heart
at the start
of break beats

She speaks prolific
her spirit monolithic
gifted tongue
singing of suns
kissing moons
while I imagine
creating sons
within her womb
becoming as one
moving in tune
with rhythmical heartbeats
bouncing off chests

Taking metered breaths
that profess
I....

love...
you...
in three part harmony
thinking of
three parts
that long to be
enveloped in
your verses
for eternities

I turn to see
us lying between
the lifetimes
creating lifelines
from the sunshine
on our skin
speaking from within
my spirit sends
messages of
parenthesis and colons

Retrieving sunsets
that was stolen
but are found
in our moments
when our hands touch
heartbeats rush...
to a pause

Make Believe Dreams

She brought me Saturn
and I sang truth
to her

Listening
as dreams occur
I defer from nights scenes
that bring back
moments of mine
that tries to define
time and space

Using my mind
and face
I place
myself at the apex
taking eight steps
that leads to heaven
but eleven to the
corridors of metaphors

My spirits soar
at the heights
of words in flight
moving at the
allusion that
my sight pictures
me nearly
on the top

of mountains
shouting that
my pen has
committed premeditated
lines
that incise
isosceles angles
and scribe obtuse
preambles
that untangle
words mangled
between the lines
that multiplies time
and divides space
which equals rhymes
that equate
to the pains that
remain ingrained

I changed the
temporary markings
on the sun
leaving my
bedrock undone
going from
terrestrial to
celestial son
using one
infinity at a time

to forever
find a present
for tomorrow

Spending time
borrowed
I loan my nights
for pawns
staying upon
mental planes
I nose dive
into five senses
of common bond

I don cloaks
of daggers
adding to a swagger
that staggers
off the right path
I left to have
peace mind
one last time

Please leave me
with the option
of watching
time stop
as my mind hops
the turnstile of infinity

and mimics the
sound of heartbeats
as these sharp
streets lacerate
feet on the road
to righteous paths

Pardon if my
laugh masks
the pain
I find shelter
from the reign
of never
that chains itself
to all that is left
reaching up
to the depths
of lost breath
I breathe
my dreams
into make believe

Moments In Time

Hands drop

We untouch
from our clutch
that we've
wanted so much
and now we
have it

Pure magic
as our lips
depart
I feel my
heart beat
in tune with
yours

it's a quarter
'til four
and I'm wanting
more time
to hold you
close

Missing you
the most
when we're
apart

I start to
walk away from you
coming in to view
is your
pretty smile
that for awhile
was my companion
at night

I can't wait
to see you
in my sight
I type
"On my way"
and press send
looking to see
my friend
who loves me
more than myself

With twenty minutes left
I think of
your picture
on the bookshelf
and wonder if
you changed your hair
If so
I wouldn't care

as long as I
see you there
I'll be a happy man

Walking past a
white van
too close to my
car door
I'll ignore this
inconvenience for
the moment

I just looked at
the phone when
you sent me your text
laughing under my breath
I pull out and turn
left on the intersection

Thinking of the session
we shared in
our last encounter
a little less than
an hour to go
stuck in traffic
so slow
listening to "Love T.K.O."
puts me in a better
mood

Letting my memory
soothe my nerves
when I think of
your curves
even the words
I use cruise
backwards
in time
with you
stuck on my mind

The Dopest Thing I Ever Saw

I ain't never saw
nothing this dope
until I saw you

Beaming so beautiful
my oracle
blowing truth
through wind pipes
and hitchhikes
through life
with outstretched thumbs
as she hums
"Going up to Yonder"

I ponder
if you came
here to
alleviate my fears
or appear
just to say
"here, taste what this is"
this girl of his
I tell me
is the dopest
thing I ever saw

'til I wrote love
and made it law

I draw conclusions
of our names
in heart halves
and I'd laugh
if I didn't think
it was this serious
delirious I'd be
when you get around me
you the
dopest thing I ever saw

When I taste your raw
sensuality
I gradually gravitate
to where our dreams
procreate destiny
and our love
reproduces truth
it's much more than
consummation
when constellations
fill my pigmentation
and my respirations
are incantations
of
I ain't never saw
nothing this dope
'til I saw you

Behind my eyes
like love
I come before you
and come true
like dreams wished
as we kiss
under shooting stars
which are ours
so we share the
sun and moon
and move in tune
with one
heartbeat

Hearing you speak
between each one
I'd give thousand
lifetimes if I can keep
just one
that'll keep
under my tongue
and taste the addition
which equals three
I's in infinity
here lies my serenity
I picture the
dopest thing I ever saw

Going as far
as our love
can take us
and make us
as one and one together
and multiply forever
by the 1st and 3rd letter
of unity...
you and I

Conquering worlds
writing love letters
that twirls
towards the sun
and shine our vows
into view still
I ain't never saw
nothing this dope
until I saw you

Uno

Break please my heart don't …

Make me says things
out of turn
skip
reverse
back to you
again I go

Backwards or
head first
it seems
I should've
looked twice
or spake your name
thrice
in the mirror
looking four times
for your reflection
to appear
but I didn't
this time

No time spent
listening to
echoes in my mind
that I used to
pretend
I didn't hear

but I did hear them
ring clear
and I'd look
over my shoulder
caused I feared that
fear would come
around the corner
often
in pairs

One time
I caught them
eavesdropping
in on one
of my conversations
it was like
they were waiting
for Jealously and Anger
to add their
two cents in
and I thought it was
nonsense until when
it all made sense
and then
the echoes
started getting louder
again

Then I
couldn't tell my own
voice from them
and they would
always call me
their friend
and say how I'd
never be lonely
again
but
they didn't stop me
from remembering when
I asked you…
My heart break please don't

But that wish
never came true
and as pitiful
as it sounded
backwards and twisted
as I mouthed it
I found it harder
to say
any other way

I couldn't dare
ask you to stay
and over and over
I heard these words

in a message
that conveyed that
"These are just games that
the heart likes to play"
so here I stand
watching night
turn into day
wishing I could
skip a turn
reverse
back to you
I go again

Drawing four ways
to remember
words I heard
you say
dive head first
into you
without a second
thought or clue
of the three things
that ring like
echoes in my mind
but I all I find
is voices speaking
three at a time
saying
Please break my heart
don't

Sunsets

In Remembrance

The love
that we possess
is far less
than what is
described

Your silhouette
by my side
provides the
closure
I need to get over
the underlying
crying performed
before your image

Our love diminished
before the final page
finished
and I grimace
at the epilogue
foreseen

Forcing the
the last gleam
of your smile
to the pile of
refuse in my mind

Counting the countless times
spent reciting
your piercing lines
tattooed on my chest

You've aborted my
last breath
and incinerated
the memories left
on my mental mantle

My hands full
of blank love letters
and notes of
"It'll get better"
written in third person
Cursing the vows
once said
still replayed in my head
as I remember
how days once were

She

She floats through
my mind
occupying each
and every space
that can be
and ever was
real

I can see her in dreams

I conjugate with her
in fantasies

I marry her with
love and hate
when I speak
of her name

This is She

She has poisoned
and purified
every ounce
of my being

I am convinced
that my last breaths
on my dying day
will be spent
on her

This is She...

These hands...
with these hands
I have caressed
and cared for
the most beautiful
and gentle being
man has ever
laid eyes upon

I ate the fruit from heaven
each time I spoke her name
I slept on
the celestial rings of Saturn

When I laid
upon her breast
I heard the pulse of mankind
beat with each step
She took

I speak of She
who has illuminated
my lips
with her anointed kiss
as She showed me
true heaven
as She and I became

one
intertwining our flesh
our lives
our destinies…
I speak of she!!!

She who has left
this indescribable void
in my heart

She!!!
who has shown me
the coldest nights
and unwavering loneliness

She!!!
whom I praise
I curse with the
same breath
and loathe with
the same lips
I speak of She

this is SHE!!!
this is SHE!!!

For Black Eyes Only

Shhhh… I want to
show something to you
only you can see

Can you see me
with bruise laden
body crudely displayed
like forgotten corpses
on metal tables?

Foreshadowing

The unraveling of
packages of hate
eating a full plate
of regret

Seconds…
of agonizing
pain screaming
my name like
It's my birthright

Clench tight fists
as hits fade
further and further
from feeling

I'm knelling
at the altar

of remorse
hailing Marys
and whatever father, sons
will hear me

I am clearly
in a battered
state
sautéed, fried
and served on a
dinner plate
for him
to devour

Looking closely
at the hour
half past midnight
is normally when
the graveyard delight
begins

Tumbling through door
wondering if he's pissed
off I whisper
prayers to pillows
muted by the angels
under the covers

He comes in
the bedroom

smothering me
with what
I wish was attention

My muscles tense when
his vodka breath
scorches my neck
I dig into what I
have left and I
escape to the before times

Before lines formed under
my eyes and
into my nose
I miss the good days
when I'd be amazed
when he didn't call
me before bedtime
to wish me sweet dreams

Now the only surreal
scenes I have are
the blue lights I
see right before
I pass out

I want to take
the trip but
maybe I took
the wrong route

As he
drools down my neck
I forgot about the
good times
and all I can
fashion in my mind
is please finish
and get this over

Seeing my dreams of
love burst like
supernovas
as he turns me
from his lover
to his prey
and I pray
that the pain
subsides soon

Living in a vacuum
of recycled love
memories that's
killing me
faster that he will
if I don't find
the will to
free myself from
this hell of disappointments

I'm anointed
by the touch
of his fist
it frees me
from the design
of the rose colored
mind I've fashioned
after trashing myself
to be in this
position

I'm wishing for
horse drawn carriages
promise fulfilled marriages
and eyes that don't
swell up in the
sunlight

My father was truly right
"you attract what you
deserve" and
with my teeth
hitting the curb
I deserve a
love that will
remember my smile
and not color with black
and blue only

like a poor child
with not enough
crayons

The day yearns for me
burning to be born
and burst free from the
anomaly that is me

Being sculpted as a fetus
an elitist with a
commoner's tastes
that tastes its own
blood way too often

Let rose petals line
my coffin
and as respects are paid
let the words heard
be conveyed that
Shhhh... I want to
show something to you
that only you can see
and let my black eyes
gaze upon your
soul for eternity

Wish I Could

Heart pierced
in a million places
walking a million
paces
trying to find
where the time
went
where love
was spent
entirely towards you

Loving you
as I do
moves me to
the point of tears
as fears
realized
and feeling paralyzed
numbed our hearts
cold

We once often told
one another
how the love
in each other
could never end
but now

.

.

.

I WISH I COULD
hold you
I WISH I COULD
hold you
I WISH I COULD
show you

.

.

.

How many endless
nights
I fight back
tears
reliving all our
blissful years
and now
what's here
is love that is
now gone

I can't go on
trying to perform
in this masquerade
the mistakes
we've made
caused our love
to fade
into memories
I carry
onto my heart

crying in the dark
on how we
grew apart

.

.

.

I WISH I COULD
hold you
I WISH I COULD
hold you
I WISH I COULD
show you

.

.

.

That my words
could console you
but that day
has passed
only to last
as long as
days gone
when one song
would bring us together

Now never
is our forever
our love severed
beyond repair

I still wish I could
show you
that I still care
but our moments
are memories
and will always
be remembered as
when she
STILL LOVED ME
She LOVED me
She LOVED me...

Monster – A Love Story

Lying in bed
with tears streaming
down face
naked
to the world
while fully clothed

Lonely in her
heart
where the first
part
the first dark
chapter was written

Started with hitting
and screaming while
thoughts of leaving
ran through mind

Ran also did time
as the slow train
brought pain
as it stopped frequently

Thinking he would
get better the lesser
he would drink
and sink lower
into this hell
she did

Often hid
in pills and sex
helps the pain
slow down
only for a moment

He came home and
had look in eyes
not seen before
She swore she'd
leave but
hope of love
lost somehow
cancelled out the cost of
the price her life
has paid

Laid down on bed
in head wondering
how next moments
will happen

Ask him
what's wrong
to receive
slap on face
and erased all
notions of love
as he climbs above

gripping hand
on neck
thinking this is
the worse yet
to expect what's next
would be preposterous

This monster is
tearing at flesh
ripping more than
self-respect
even death cannot
forget this tragedy

Her humanity savagely
ripped to shreds
left on bed
remembering he once
said
he loved her

Melancholy Rose

She laid shivering
I'm spinning
in my mind
actions and reactions
to help the pain
subside

Trying to hide
the pain and tears
that spill from
my eyelids
torn apart
but trying to
be that pillar
for her…

Her name is Rose
as lovely as the flower
even as sweet
it didn't take long
for me to fall in
love like
matters of emotions
writing devotions
and one page phrases
that occupy my mind
in time…

We engaged in love
no thought
of the consequence
bathing in benevolence
living a dream
like it was heaven sent
young and in love
not caring
about a future
that doesn't involve her
or us
the trust
we had was unimaginable

Rose 19
and I at 22
we had already grew
to a point where
we couldn't be apart
then the morning sickness
starts and
she tells me
she's late
and I'm
trying not to panic

Rose is looking to me
and I'm the furthest
from direction

the time passes
and depression is
leaking in
the only solution
is one I never thought
I'd be pondering

One early Thursday
us sitting in
the waiting room
hands trembling
trying to think of
more consoling words
her name called
she looks back at me
for a glimmer of hope
I stare back blankly
nothing to offer
but more hopelessness

What am I doing?

*How can we
take the life
of an unborn child?*

*God, it's too late!
We should have
went another way*

My mind spinning
filled with remorse
and guilt harboring
prayers leaves my mouth

She comes out later
arms folded
staring at the floor
sobbing quietly
like her soul
has just been
stolen from her

I run and hold her
no words said
just my caress
we break down
nothing left but
past happiness

Sad Hours

Time spent between
now and half past
forever
tends to sever
the cord between
love and
my ability to breathe

This heart fallen from
my sleeve leaves
no trace or
remembrance
no semblance of
the man I was

Withered and frayed
lie the petals
of my love's bloom
beckoning for death
to come soon
to rescue me
in flaming chariot
yet hung by
fate's lariat

This cross
I carry it
and bear love's thorns
as my crown

the sound of my tears
feels like years
added to my sentence
in this hell

My body the cell
to which I am
confined to reminders of
what love I once
had
these long hours
are sad
and time's hands
remain still

Missed Opportunity

Entered my life at difficult period you did

Conceded and confused was I

Still stuck in
shenanigans and immaturity

Misused trust I
simply fucked and
walked my way
not considering yours

I never listened to problems
or
visited while you were sick

I laughed when you said you'd leave

I walked off while you were crying

I got drunk on birthdays with my niggas

I went to strip clubs on Valentines

Held knife to neck once you did while sleeping

Paid no mind to your trembling hands
and running mascara down face

I knew you loved me

I knew your heart

Pure…innocent…mine

I scoffed at family notions

Abortions two

Sorry I didn't feel

Sunday morning
mind clarity and conscious building

Guilt remorse heart feeling

Plans to make amends

Called phone no answer

Outside heavy downpour

Hours past, worry builds
Peering out window

Voice mailbox full

Phone rings…

Friend on other end frantic

Sentences incomplete…sobs and cries

News broken in pieces

Head on collision on interstate

No survivors found

Description made

Phone dropped

Mind in shambles…

Believing In Forever

She told me
that she
didn't believe
in forever

That I should
let her
tether on the
wings of never
got that chance
to say
I love you

But I do
through the
letters I send
when you let
me within
your soul

I compose
words so
beautiful
I told them
to angels
and angled
my smile
to the sun
that is only

mentioning one
of the infinities
that I mentally scribed
behind my eyes

I cried
when you said
I love you
but your words
didn't get to
reach their
destination

I can feel
the frustration
in our communication
when I'm facing
spoken dreams
that's figments
of my imagination

I'm pacing
back and forth
for the forth
and fifth time
trying the find
the right line
that shows
that I love you

But fairy tales
don't come true
and with you
my happy ever afters
tend to
come after
my far, far aways
where you seem
to stay

I remember
hearing you say that
you don't believe
in forever
and never comes
around too damn soon
and why thoughts
of you come
when I look at the moon

I assume
it's because I only
see you in quarters
and I thought of
ways to make change
but the fact still
remains
that you don't believe

in forever
but have you ever
been in love
now

The Book of Naomi

She looks out the window
hoping he comes home soon

He's gone mostly
no whereabouts
no phone calls often

Ready to leave him
thinking he's
probably out fucking
or flirting with bitches

Stressed out
she cries frequently
wondering why he
hits her repeatedly

With liquor on his breath
is only when he wants sex
She has
called police often
only to drop the charges later
lets him back in
and starts the whole cycle again

Two miscarriages
third try...
maybe a baby boy
four months pregnant

not wanting abortion
nor single parenting
yet she's finding hair again
on pillowcases
and woven into his clothes
light brown
and her hair jet-black

Smell of pussy
and perfume on him
creeps in late nights
hides his cell phone
signs are telltale
but naïve as hell

not seeing it
believing it for what it is

Lost and distraught
searching for answers
needing love and affection
that she thought she had
now a broken memory

Too in love with being in love
she's trapped in a cycle
like infinity
random indecision
fear of losing

the only love she's ever known
hoping he'll change
when baby comes

Not wanting a life without him
can't stand the life with him
sobs and tears
pain not equaling her years
she has to choose…

Shoot Straight

Just shoot straight
aiming straight for
my chest
without a second
thought to
what happens next

Let go of
regrets when
you release your
bow and
go to where
my love
needs you
the most

Come as close
to my last
breath as you
can and
let a million
lifetimes span
in each spin
as your words
go within
piercing my passion

I'm asking you
to do

what can't wait
and shoot straight
aim for my name
and I'll call
out God
as I remain
between heaven
and you

Let your words
go through
to tomorrow
and follow
good wishes
and I pray
that what misses
is not what
you hold in
your hand

Flow like
sands in the
glasses of hours
and let this be
ours like
our first kiss
was

Be careful
because your
target is a
promise that I
need you to keep
so when your words
go deep
let them speak
to my heart

Close your eyes
and aim in the dark
and part yesterday
and the day after
with a chapter
that's nearing the close

Her eyes froze
into mine
trying to find
the right words
then eyes blurred
with tears

You have nothing
to fear
just shoot straight

and come as near
to my soul
as you can
if you miss
shoot again
and then
witness
what occurs
when my heart is
filled with the
words of…
Her

Be like your
verbs and
let the action
of this passion
happen
like I'm crashing
into dreams
while wide awake
all I need you
to do
is
just shoot straight

Broken Promise

I promise
I'll come back for you

I saw you
beaten down
like ancient brick
monoliths

Reciting scripts
that read
hold me
tight to your
chest and
don't look back

Yet instead
I wept when
the rain stopped
I sobbed as
the sun shined
because I would
go back to that
place in my
mind where I
heard you and
that same sound is
what I hear
in my nightmares
and I don't
sleep that often

I need you
to wait for me

Housed in bottles
broken yet
empty still yet
filled with
these dreams I can't
touch but
they feel damn
real to me
it's almost as if
you see me
walking into nightmares
swallowing sleep
'til I can't breathe
but still I
can't grab your hand

I need to go
but I promise
I'll be back

If I could still
have your hand
to lead me
through rose gardens
I know I
wouldn't be

harboring these
dreams that come
much harder when
I walk through here
alone

These thorns cause
wounds that heal slow
and these wounds
don't come from
the kind of hurting
you know but
I know they still
bleed the same way
as before
I remember how
you bled that day
and all I remember
was that I needed
to say
I swear that
I won't leave

*I will never
leave you alone*

But I needed
you to believe
that I could

take you back home
one day
but deep down
I wanted to say
don't trust me
because I don't
know the way back
home and
my eyes had
cried for so long
and this emptiness
has been prolonged
because I thought
that what I
did was right
but instead
I left you alone
and now
all I feel is wrong
and I don't know
where else
to go

These rose bushes
don't grow
where we lived
I remember where we
lived as kids but
I don't remember that

we lived
but I dreamed that
we did live
once upon a time
didn't we?

The Unspoken Word

The words that used
to come so easy
fail me in a time
when I need to be
purging my soul
on loose leaf
filled with lines
of grief that
blur under tear stains
all that remains
are lines that go
unfinished
and diminished
sentences
that fails to replenish
my heart that beats
a muted tune

Hoping that
words will come soon
to soothe me
and remove me
from this state
not bearing the
strength to wait
for _ _ _ _
soon come
knowing I'm far
from the place

which cradled grace
highlighted _ _ _
face

My joy has
been replaced
with a taste
that has left my
entire being bitter
this is my sorrowful winter
this heartless December
that centers its fangs
onto my soul
there is no warmth
from this cold
no beauty to behold
no release from the control
of _ _ _ _
which has left me
this shell
in this unrelenting hell
of a pain I know
all too well

Residing within
me so hideously
and persistently
piercing my side
under this crown

of thorns
I hide
from the pain
that remains
unchanged
called _ _ _ _

Tonight

Tonight I will delight
in your moon waves
and paint ways
to say I love you
onto tomorrow
and borrow
the memories
from today
to make way
for next morning
and I'm yearning
for tonight

Let's you and I
write manifestos
in Braille cursive
and tip Earth
when we connect
like the words I kept
in the love letters
I slept next to
and let tonight
begin the flight
to ever afters and
compose unending
chapters that begin
with a kiss and
contain gifts between
your lips

I lift daydreams
into day scenes
and night pictures
and whisper motions
under starlights

Hold on tight
to me and breathe
like your breath
was my song
and your words
were the melody
my heart danced to
'til dawn
and when the nights
moves on
let the trails
that set sail
in the sky
lead me to tomorrow
where I
hope to find you
where I saw you last

Take my hand and grasp
as if the last midnight
was tonight
and lets kiss like
it's 11:59

If I could take time
and hold you
like 60 seconds
were mine
and I'd leave
us with just
10 to begin
to spin you love poems
and write 9
down the curve of
your spine and define
8 ways to make
this taste stay
as sweet in my mind
as it is in your lips
and count 7
steps to bliss
and the heaven sent
gift between your hips
that makes me dive in
and deep 6
all 5 of your senses
and since it's
little time for
4 play
let's come before
I say 3 things
that convey the
time left in our hands

"Don't let go"
2 hearts
joining as 1
chasing after
shaded suns
knowing that
tonight
will never come

The First Goodbye

Breathe…

Breath as if the
wind were whispers
and my voice
was a familiar
friend

Tend to my callings
and send me
away smiling

Blow kisses
onto my eyelids
as I envision
tomorrow through
your yesterday
touches

Clutch us like
we're tearing apart
and write love letters
in the dark
so that they
mean more
in the daylight

Breathe with me
gently whispering

happily ever afters
and know that
we knew love
once upon a time

Remind me
about love
and refresh
memories through
your caress and regrets
would not dare
to follow

Empty my heart
until it's hollow
and pour into it
once more
those nights
that I forgot
that I'd never forget

Tell me of
promises kept
and keep them
in safe keeping

Tell me of
forever evenings
and mornings

where the sun
rises every hour

Remember how
once our
names together
itself sounded like
poetry
and flowed as three
rivers
joining at six bends
and we pretend
that it was us
sailing into
infinity

Remember me
as I dedicated
days to you
and nights
to us

Shaking the dust
from forever
to make today
seem brand new

Bring our dreams
into view

and place them
upon mantles
that slows the
earth
to a stand still
looking at such
a beautiful display
which makes this
even harder to say
...goodbye...

Outro

In through
the out door
I go again

Trying to put ends
on things that have yet
to begin and
starting to manifest spins
I don't want to stop

Push
Play
me over and over again
hear me say words
I only spoke
in my sleep

Out stretching my hand
but alas, you're so deep
into me I can't reach
you

Touch…
Touch my fingertips please

Show me that
you are real
and that this
reel to reel
reveals something more
than I can feel

Touch…
Touch me as if
passing and if
glancing is all
we can do
then walk slow
for me

Speak to me
with each step taken
and I'll take in each
breath and
pick up all that
you've left for me,
Right?

Must be

Must be right
for me to hear
your echoes in
the shadows of
sunrises
and find your fingerprints
beneath sunrays,
Right?

It has to be

It has to be like
your voice written
in calligraphy
because only words
by you could look
this beautiful

See, it would
have to be etched
in my flesh because
only thoughts of you
can get under my skin
like this

This one
counted as two times
a blessing
and heard for third
because a single word
from your mouth
is strong enough
for us begin four play

Stop
Rewind
to a time
when my mind
orbited around

lines I could weave
that would fit on
your skin perfect
and when shooting stars
pressed against flesh
you knew it was
my signature
with the date and time
left blank
because I could not
write history in motion
but I could pen devotions
that swept across
your face like minute hands
and hours would be spent
jealous of the sands
that flowed through your
looking glass

Looking past the out door
wanting to go in again
and spin you
words that you
once knew and
write you poems
that you could
dream to and
revolve through doors
that allowed me

to see you
once more
and twice again

In through the
out door I go again
putting the ends
on things
that have yet to begin
but beautiful still
even though
they're just pretend

www.ingramcontent.com/pod-product-compliance
Lightning Source LLC
Chambersburg PA
CBHW072003040426
42447CB00009B/1472